MW01617717

Tell me about...

The United Nations

Foreword by Kofi A. Annan

Secretary-General of the United Nations

Text by Jean-Jacques Chevron

Translated from the French by Vera Kalm

NOUVELLE ARCHE DE NOE EDITIONS ©
153, boulevard Haussmann – 75008 PARIS (France)
Phone : +33 (0)1 53 83 95 78 – Fax : +33 (0)1 53 75 36 80
E-mail : nan-editions@wanadoo.fr
Web site : www.nan-editions.com

ACKNOWLEDGMENTS

The publisher wishes to express his gratitude to the following for their valuable contributions and assistance:

UNITED NATIONS HEADQUARTERS, NEW YORK
Office of the Secretary-General
Department of Public Information
Office for the Coordination of Humanitarian Affairs

UNITED NATIONS OFFICE AT GENEVA
Information Service and Library

UNITED NATIONS INFORMATION CENTRE, PARIS

THE MINISTRY OF FOREIGN AFFAIRS, PARIS

■

2nd edition (for the english version)
Printed in France – October 2002
for Nouvelle Arche de Noé Editions

Illustrations: Emmanuel Soren; Cover: Laurent Elcé
Graphic designer : Joffrin / Paris

Photos: © UN: M. Claude, Y. Nagata Ara, J. Isaac, M. Grant, P.S. Sudhakaran, E. Schneider, A. Brizzi, E. Kanalstein, S. Whitehouse, S. Bemeniev.

« Collection du citoyen », based on an idea of Jean-Loup Mayol

Copyright: 10 / 02
Law No.49-956 of 16.7.1949 on publications for young people.

2002, Nouvelle Arche de Noé Editions – ISBN 2-84368-021-2

Glossary of Terms

Apartheid: A rigid policy of segregation of the non-white population under the former Government in the Republic of South Africa.

Committee: A group of delegates meeting to discuss specific issues and to prepare resolutions.

Consensus: Agreement arrived at between a number of people. In the UN it is agreement between all Member States.

Constitution: A system of fundamental principles of law according to which a nation – or an organization – is governed. The Charter is the constitution of the UN.

Convention: An international agreement dealing with a specific matter.

Genocide: The deliberate and systematic extermination of a national, ethnic or religious group.

Good offices: Influence exerted by a person in a position of power in settling a dispute.

Mediation: An attempt to bring about agreement or reconciliation between opponents in a dispute.

Multilateral diplomacy: The conduct of negotiations and other relations involving the participation of several nations.

Resolutions: Texts through which the organs of the United Nations transmit their decisions (in the case of the Security Council) or their recommendations (General Assembly or ECOSOC) to Member States and the organizations of the UN system.

Session: A period during which a series of meetings is held.

Subsidiary organs: Committees specialized in certain areas, subordinate to a main body and constituted to prepare decisions or recommendations for its review.

Supranational power: Power beyond the authority of national Governments.

Table of contents

UNITED NATIONS  NATIONS UNIES

It gives me great pleasure to introduce to you a book that I hope will serve as a guide to anyone – young or not so young – who wants to learn more about the United Nations.

Tell me about the United Nations gives a simple, clear and concise account of the history and work of the United Nations. Today, that work covers a broader range than ever before. With the end of the Cold War, the terrifying arsenal of missiles and bombs built up over the course of half a century has been reduced. There is a new willingness among the nations of the world to cooperate, and new confidence about what they can achieve.

But this new era has also brought with it new problems: political systems unravelling, States breaking up, old national rivalries reawakening, ethnic, religious, social and linguistic tensions threatening to escalate into violent conflict.

Globalization, while bringing us closer together, has also reinforced inequalities between the haves and have-nots. Civil wars are forcing millions to flee their homes; pollution is destroying the environment; the drug problem is destroying young people; AIDS is wrecking families and communities.

To build true peace and security throughout the world, we must ensure the human security of every person. That means the security of food, shelter and health care, but also the right to education, to freedom of expression, to vote and to take part in decision-making. In short, it means guaranteeing all human rights for all.

The UN has no greater mission than that. To achieve it, we must use all our imagination and common sense – attributes we have been able to develop over more than half a century.

But we cannot do it alone. We need the support of people everywhere. That is why we seek to build awareness among citizens – especially young people like you, who represent the future. It is my sincere hope that all who read this book will understand how useful – indispensable, even – our institution is, but also the complexity of challenges before it. And I hope, finally, that it will inspire every reader to think about ways of contributing to the work of building a better world for all.

Kofi A. Annan
Secretary-General of the United Nations

Determined

to save succeeding generations from the scourge of war, which twice in our lifetime has brought untold sorrow to mankind, **and to** reaffirm faith in fundamental human rights, in the dignity and worth of the human person, in the equal rights of men and women and of nations large and small, **and to** establish conditions under which justice and respect for the obligations arising from treaties and other sources of international law can be maintained, **and to** promote social progress and better standards of life in larger freedom,

And for these ends

to practice tolerance and live together in peace with one another as good neighbours, **and to** unite our strength to maintain international peace and security, **and to** ensure, by the acceptance of principles and the institution of methods, that armed force shall not be used, save in the common interest, **and to** employ international machinery for the promotion of the economic and social advancement of all peoples,

Have resolved to combine our efforts to accomplish these aims

Accordingly, our respective Governments, through representatives assembled in the city of San Francisco, who have exhibited their full powers found to be in good and due form, have agreed to the present Charter of the United Nations and do hereby establish an international organization to be known as the United Nations.

Preamble to the Charter of the United Nations
Published by the United Nations Department of Public Information, Photographs and Exhibits Section.

In September 2000, five years after commemorating with pride the fiftieth anniversary of its founding, the United Nations adopted a landmark document, the Millennium Declaration. It contains the solemn commitment of all the Member States to devote the first 15 years of our new century to bring about significant improvements in the lives of people around the world by putting an end to extreme poverty and hunger, widespread illiteracy and disease.

A little background...

The United Nations (UN), is a complex, somewhat mythical world which serves as the meeting-ground for political powers from around the world. It is unique among international institutions, considering the vast array of tasks entrusted to it. The UN is involved in all aspects of human activity; it therefore plays an important role in the international community, in spite of the inadequate human and financial resources at its disposal.

The birth of the United Nations

In 1945, the countries that emerged victorious from the greatest armed conflict in history proclaimed their resolve "to save succeeding generations from the scourge of war, which twice in our lifetime has brought untold sorrow to mankind". This solemn declaration opens the Preamble to the Charter of the United Nations.

After the end of the First World War, there was an initial attempt to secure the preservation of peace by creating an international organization, the League of Nations. Unfortunately, the League did not succeed in attracting the full participation of all the nations of the world and its founders were unable to stop the totalitarian powers whose actions brought about the outbreak of the second, most disastrous armed conflict of this century.

View of the illuminated United Nations building in New York, marking the fiftieth anniversary of the Organization in 1995.

The role of the United Nations

Facing a world in ruins after the Second World War, the "United Nations" – so named by Franklin D. Roosevelt, war-time President of the United States – declared its faith in fundamental human rights, justice, social progress and the value and dignity of the individual.

Those nations committed themselves to unite to live together in peace. Their Governments thus decided to create a great new organization, which would be strong and universal and which would enable them to achieve their goal of world peace. Such an institution would provide them with a forum for discussing the problems facing people around the world and for finding ways together to help in their resolution.

The Charter of the United Nations was signed by 51 countries in June of 1945, in San Francisco (USA).

The objectives of the United Nations

The United Nations was founded on 24 October 1945. The Charter is, in a practical sense, its constitution*. It sets out the rights and duties of the States that are to become its members and provides the structure for the functioning of the new institution.

The major objectives of the UN are:

- To maintain peace and international security;
- To develop friendly relations among nations;
- To implement international cooperation in the economic, social, cultural and humanitarian fields;
- To promote respect for human rights and fundamental freedoms;
- To establish a centre where Member States can work together to achieve these common objectives.

The five major objectives of the United Nations.

■ *Who are the members of the United Nations?*

In September 2002 the United Nations welcomed its 191st Member State. It now comprises all the independent countries on our planet.

In 1945, after the end of World War II, these numbered only 51. Over the next fifty years, however, an ever growing number of nations gained their independence and freedom of action - through peace treaties, or decolonization , (as in Africa and Asia), or the disintegration of large political entities (such as the former Soviet Union and Yugoslavia).

All were keen to join the vast and expanding international community of the United Nations as full members. Even those countries most determined to maintain their neutrality, like Switzerland, or some small island countries, in the Antilles or the Pacific Ocean, came to recognize that they could not remain outside an organization which was becoming truly universal.

By joining, States solemnly pledge to fulfill the duties defined by the Charter, above all to try to settle their differences by peaceful means. They also agree to assist the Organization in any activity undertaken in accordance with the provisions of the Charter.

Did you know that...

The Holy See chose to send only a permanent observer to the United Nations, despite the fact that the Vatican has the status of a State.

■ *So, what is the United Nations?*

Although it flies a flag with the globe as its emblem, the UN is not a "super-State", nor is it a world government. The buildings of the UN and the land they occupy are, however, international territory. The UN has its own security guards and its own radio and television services, which broadcast all over the world. It also has its own post office and issues its own postage stamps.

But the States members of the UN remain sovereign and equal and have no intention of delegating this sovereignty to any supranational* entity. The United Nations is **a forum, a permanent centre where discussions and diplomatic negotiations take place and where international decisions are made.**

The Palais des Nations (Palace of Nations),
seat of the United Nations Office at Geneva, Switzerland.

Did you know that...

The great, majestic building inherited from the League of Nations, the Palais des Nations in Geneva, is also the venue of countless year-round international meetings and negotiations which are of the utmost importance for peace and for development.

At the United Nations, representatives of almost all the countries on earth, rich and poor, large and small, strong and weak, with varying political and social systems, can have a say on all the problems facing the world. They come together either in large international gatherings or in more technical working committees*, or even in small groups without official designation, where negotiations often have a better chance of succeeding than in meetings where the public is present.

Did you know that...

In a large number of countries, especially in developing regions of the world, UN representatives, the Resident Coordinators, oversee technical cooperation, humanitarian assistance and emergency relief programmes.

■ *Where does the UN work?*

The Headquarters of the UN has been located in New York (USA) since 1947, but the Organization has other important offices elsewhere as well: in Geneva (Switzerland), Vienna (Austria), Addis Ababa (Ethiopia), Nairobi (Kenya), Bangkok (Thailand), Amman (Jordan) and Santiago (Chile).

In addition, there are UN Information Centres in the capital cities of many countries. Their task is to make the work of the United Nations known to the general public, various professional circles and the media.

Member States, in turn, appoint ambassadors to the UN. These "Permanent Representatives", assisted by teams of diplomats and experts in various fields, take part in the work of the Organization all year long. Heads of State or Government, or ministers responsible for specialized areas, usually join them for major debates or "summit meetings".

Delegates to the United Nations are not part of the Organization's staff. They represent their respective countries.

■ *What languages are used at the UN?*

The official languages of the United Nations are Arabic, Chinese, English, French, Russian and Spanish. In all official meetings there is simultaneous interpretation of speeches and translation of documents into these languages.

Did you know that...

In the daily life of the Organization, English and French are the working languages of the Secretariat.

Aerial view of UN Headquarters in New York.

How does the UN function?

A number of bodies enable the Organization to carry out its activities. They have been established by the Charter of the United Nations. They are the General Assembly, the Security Council, the Economic and Social Council, the International Court of Justice and the Secretariat. The Trusteeship Council, having been created to supervise the administration of former Trust Territories, completed its task in 1994. At that time, all 11 Territories had attained self-government, or independence.

■ *The General Assembly*

The General Assembly is the UN's main deliberative body; all the other bodies of the Organization report to it. Its regular annual session* opens every September at UN Headquarters in New York and often extends well into the following year.

On the first day of its session the General Assembly elects a president for a term of one year, chosen from among representatives of Member States, each time from a different geographical region. Now and then the Assembly meets in special session to take up matters of particular importance.

The General Assembly is the forum where every autumn the foreign ministers of nearly all the nations of the world and a great many heads of State and Government meet to present the views of their countries on the major issues facing the international community and on the work of the Organization. Meetings of the General Assembly also offer Member States the opportunity to hold informal discussions on neutral ground and away from the limelight of official diplomatic gatherings.

Most of the work of the Assembly takes place in six main committees, specialized in different areas and open to the participation of all Member States. At the end of the session each committee submits its report and proposed resolutions* for adoption by the plenary meeting of the Assembly.

Every day nearly 3,000 diplomats meet in various committees and working groups. Indeed, the facilities offered by the United Nations for continuous international negotiations – for multilateral diplomacy* – constitute one of the most distinctive and most useful features of its work.

Each Member State has one vote at the UN, no matter what its size and political power. At the General Assembly most of the resolutions are adopted by simple majority. But there is a constant effort to reach decisions by consensus* (that is to say, adopting resolutions without having to vote), although this does not always prove possible. Member States are not compelled to implement resolutions adopted by the General Assembly; therefore, they carry more weight with Governments if they are adopted unanimously.

Did you know that...

A Member State that fails to pay its contribution to the UN budget may lose its right to vote at the General Assembly.

THE GENERAL ASSEMBLY IN SESSION.

The fight against drug abuse was the subject of a special session of the General Assembly in 1998.

The General Assembly has a vast mandate.

It discusses a wide range of issues concerning the maintenance of international peace and security; the cooperation between States in the political area; the development of international law; the protection and promotion of human rights; collaboration in the economic, social and cultural domain; and emergency situations.

It approves the Organization's budget; elects the members of the Security Council and of the Economic and Social Council; and appoints the Secretary-General on the recommendation of the Security Council.

The agenda of the General Assembly is therefore always extremely heavy; it includes more than 150 items every year.

Did you know that...

The Security Council also makes recommendations to the General Assembly on the admission of new members to the UN and on the nomination of the Secretary-General.

MEETING OF THE SECURITY COUNCIL.

The Security Council

The Charter gives the Security Council primary responsibility for the maintenance of international peace and security. It is the most important political organ of the UN and is best known to the general public. It can be convened at any time, when the need arises.

The Council has 15 members. Five of them, the major victorious powers of the Second World War (China, France, the Russian Federation, the United Kingdom and the United States), are permanent members. The other ten are elected from among Member States on a rotating basis for a term of two years. The presidency of the Council changes every month and is assumed by each Council member in turn.

While the other bodies of the UN can only make recommendations to Governments, decisions of the Security Council are binding on Member States. The decisions of the Council, called resolutions, must be adopted by at least nine of the 15 votes of its membership. A resolution cannot pass over the negative vote of one of the permanent members.

The principal mandate of the Security Council is to examine any situation that could involve a threat to peace or lead to a conflict between nations; recommend means for a peaceful settlement of disputes; invite members to impose economic sanctions to prevent aggression; and, if necessary, agree on military measures.

When a threat to international peace is brought before it, the Council always seeks to find a peaceful solution to the conflict that has arisen. The States involved in the conflict are invited to participate in the Council's discussions, even if they are not members, but they do not have the right to vote. The Council may itself investigate a situation and undertake mediation* between the parties or it may ask the Secretary-General to offer his "good offices"*.

If any one of the five permanent members of the Council is opposed to a resolution and votes against it, the resolution is automatically rejected. This is called exercising their veto power.

Did you know that...

When armed conflicts occur, the Security Council seeks to find ways to end the fighting as quickly as possible. It may call for a cease-fire or send peace-keeping forces to the area – the "Blue Helmets" – under the United Nations flag.

The Economic and Social Council

The Economic and Social Council, better known by its acronym, ECOSOC, plays a central role in reviewing the economic and social activities of the UN, its bodies dealing with operational programmes, and the specialized agencies, which together form the UN "System".

ECOSOC examines reports of these organizations and adopts recommendations – "resolutions" – on issues affecting the international community in the economic, social, cultural, educational and health fields, among others. These resolutions are intended to guide Member States and the organizations of the UN system in their work.

Did you know that...

ECOSOC has 54 members, elected by the General Assembly from among the members of the UN, to serve for three years. It holds two sessions a year, alternating between New York and Geneva.

Throughout the year, the work of ECOSOC is carried out by a large number of subsidiary organs* which report to it.

The ECOSOC is, moreover, the link between the UN and over 2,500 international non-governmental organizations (NGOs). These are private associations of recognized technical standing which the UN may consult or engage in its work.

DECEMBER 11, 2001 : AWARD OF THE NOBEL PEACE PRIZE

SECRETARY-GENERAL KOFI A. ANNAN AND MR HAN-SEUNG-SOO, PRESIDENT OF THE GENERAL ASSEMBLY, HOLD THE NOBEL PEACE PRIZE AWARDED TO THE UNITED NATIONS AND TO ITS SECRETARY-GENERAL.

The International Court of Justice

The International Court of Justice is the tribunal of the United Nations. Its seat is in the Hague (Netherlands). Member States - not their citizens acting individually - may refer matters to it on which they have legal differences. The Court may also give advisory opinions on legal questions referred to it by the United Nations itself and the specialized agencies of the UN System.

The International Court of Justice in The Hague (Netherlands).

Up to year 2002, the Court had delivered 74 judgements on disputes such as land frontiers and maritime boundaries, territorial sovereignty, the non-use of force, non-interference in the internal affairs of States, hostage-taking, the right of asylum, nationality, rights of passage and economic rights. In 2002, 24 cases were pending before the Court.

The Court consists of 15 judges, all of different nationalities, chosen for their qualifications. They do not represent their governments but are independent magistrates. They are elected by the General Assembly and the Security Council to serve for nine years.

Did you know that...

Some international treaties or Conventions* provide for the Court's intervention in case of litigation.

The International Court of Justice in session in The Hague (Netherlands).

Did you know that...

The Secretariat is currently composed of about 14,800 staff members from about 170 Member States deployed all over the world. By comparison, the County of Stockholm (Sweden) has 57,000 employees.

The Secretariat

The Secretariat is the executive organ of the Organization. It is composed of professional staff, recruited internationally, who may be assigned to work at UN Headquarters or anywhere else in the world. Support staff is hired locally.

All must take an oath not to seek or receive instruction from any Government or report on their activities to any authority outside the UN.

The administrative structure of the Secretariat is very diversified and the tasks of the UN civil servants are as wide-ranging as the areas in which the Organization works.

In general, certain categories of staff are hired through competitive examinations, organized in the member countries of the UN. Beyond excellent professional qualifications, candidates are required to be fluent in one or several of the official languages of the Organization.

Under the overall direction of the Secretary-General, the Secretariat carries out the day-to-day work of the various departments of the Organization and provides the support staff needed by all the policy-making organs of the UN.

In filling the so called "professional" posts, the UN must also bear in mind the right of each Member State to have nationals on the staff (applying the principle of geographical distribution in international civil service). Consequently at times some nationalities are more sought after.

The rule does not apply to the recruitment of experts in technical cooperation, interpreters or translators, or to administrative staff of the so called "general service" category. The latter are hired in the countries where UN offices are located, for clerical work, maintenance and security.

The Secretary-General

The key individual in this structure is the Secretary-General of the United Nations. He is the highest official of the Organization and is its personification in the eyes of the world. He is the head of all UN civil servants and disposes of a sizeable staff to assist him in managing this great institution.

Unlike his predecessors, who have all been in politics or in the diplomatic service of their Governments before becoming Secretary-General, Mr. Kofi Annan spent his entire professional career within the UN system, which he entered in 1962.

Indeed, the Secretary-General has ultimate responsibility for all the activities of the UN and, at the same time, is the principal partner in discussions with the Governments of Member States. He has frequent consultations with their leaders and their Permanent Representatives, as well as with leading international personalities, at UN Headquarters and during his many visits to countries around the globe.

The Secretary-General is appointed by the General Assembly, on the recommendation of the Security Council, for a term of five years. He must be a diplomat of outstanding qualities, a personality of great sensitivity to global problems, vision, determination and faith in the ideals enshrined in the Charter of the United Nations. And, with all this, he must also be a good manager.

The kind of leadership the Secretary-General provides has an effect on the way in which the Organization works to improve the state of affairs in the world. The Secretary-General must rise above political differences and remain impartial under all circumstances. He can, if he deems fit, bring a problem to the Security Council himself.

Mr. Kofi Annan (Ghana) succeeded Mr. Boutros Boutros-Ghali (Egypt) on 1 January 1997 and was reappointed in 2001 to a second term of office ending on December 31, 2006. Previously, he held important positions within the Organization, in the fields of humanitarian assistance, peace-keeping and administration. He therefore knows "the house" inside out. His outstanding qualities as a diplomat are widely recognized.

TRYGVE LIE
(NORWAY)
1946-1953

In 2001, Mr Kofi Annan and the United Nations received the Nobel Peace Prize (*see photograph p.18*). In conferring the Prize, the Nobel Committee declared that the Secretary-General "had been pre-eminent in bringing new life to the Organization".

In also conferring the Prize on the world body, the Committee wished "to proclaim that the only negotiable road to global peace and cooperation goes by the way of the United Nations".

DAG HAMMARSKJOLD
(SWEDEN)
1953-1961

U THANT
(MYANMAR)
1962-1971

KURT WALDHEIM
(AUSTRIA)
1972-1981

JAVIER PEREZ DE CUELLAR
(PERU)
1982-1991

BOUTROS BOUTROS-GHALI
(EGYPT)
1992-1996

KOFI A. ANNAN
(GHANA)
FROM 1 JANUARY 1997

■ *Operational programmes*

Over the years, several operational programmes were established, specifically designed for direct action in countries, most often developing countries, where urgent assistance was necessary.

These programmes have their own decision-making bodies and budgets, but their directors and staff remain under the authority of the Secretary-General. The main programmes are the United Nations Development Programme (UNDP); the United Nations High Commissioner for Refugees (UNHCR); the United Nations Children's Fund (UNICEF); the World Food Programme (WFP); the United Nations Population Fund (UNFPA); and the United Nations Environment Programme (UNEP).

THE UNITED NATIONS SYSTEM (SIMPLIFIED STRUCTURE)

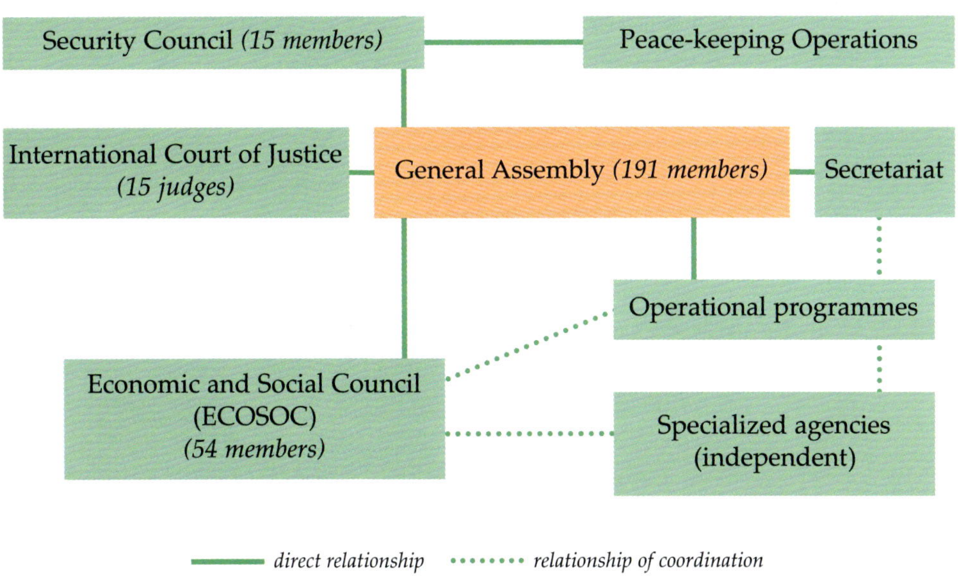

The United Nations "System"

The specialized agencies are linked to the UN by special agreements; they collaborate with each other and with the UN through a number of coordinating bodies.

The United Nations is at the centre of a large network of international organizations, called specialized agencies by the Charter. These are intergovernmental organizations, their members are States, not individuals.

Each agency has its own field of competence, ranging from labour to public health, from education to food and agriculture, from meteorology to telecommunications.

The activities of the agencies are extremely varied. They involve the establishment of international standards leading to the harmonization of national legislations; technical cooperation with developing countries; coordination of large-scale programmes at the regional and global levels; research, dissemination of information and publications; and so on.

INTERNATIONAL ATOMIC ENERGY AGENCY.

The agencies vary in size. Some have a staff of a few hundred, others a few thousand. All have their own governing bodies, independent of the UN. Each organization also has its own secretariat and budget, enabling it to function autonomously.

INTERNATIONAL MONETARY FUND.

Each is, however, linked to the UN by special agreement and all work together towards the achievement of common objectives. Along with the UN they form the UN "System", or the UN "family" of organizations.

They meet regularly within the framework of ECOSOC to discuss major issues and trends affecting their programmes.

INTERNATIONAL FUND FOR AGRICULTURAL DEVELOPMENT.

The agencies also consult with each other and with the United Nations in the UN System Chief Executives Board for Coordination on all technical and administrative aspects of their activities.

The Specialized Agencies

International Labour Organization
ILO (Geneva)

Food and Agriculture Organization of the United Nations
FAO (Rome)

United Nations Educational, Scientific and Cultural Organization
UNESCO (Paris)

World Health Organization
WHO (Geneva)

International Civil Aviation Organization
ICAO (Montreal)

Universal Postal Union
UPU (Berne)

International Telecommunication Union
ITU (Geneva)

World Meteorological Organization
WMO (Geneva)

International Maritime Organization
IMO (London)

World Intellectual Property Organization
WIPO (Geneva)

United Nations Industrial Development Organization
UNIDO (Vienna)

In addition, there are other autonomous intergovernmental organizations within the UN System: the International Atomic Energy Agency, (IAEA) in Vienna, which has a distinctive character; and the financial institutions which have assumed growing importance in activities of cooperation between industrialized and developing countries: the World Bank Group (WB) and the International Monetary Fund (IMF), both located in Washington, D.C. Then there is the International Fund for Agricultural Development (IFAD) in Rome, whose mission it is to help improve agricultural production in the poorest countries. The World Trade Organization (WTO), in Geneva, was established to oversee international trade. Although it is connected to the United Nations by a special agreement, WTO is not part of the UN System.

At the International Labour Organization, worker and employer delegations have a seat at the table, alongside Government representatives of Member States, in all decision-making bodies.

What is the purpose of the United Nations?

■ *International action*

If the structure of the UN system seems complex, it is mainly due to the fact that in every instance the international community had to "invent" the means to tackle the problems as they arose.

When the scope of these problems warrant the urgent and special attention of the world, the UN convenes global conferences to work out action plans with recommendations for Member States and the Organization itself.

Important international issues are first discussed at Headquarters, by the UN's main political bodies: the General Assembly, ECOSOC and the Security Council.

Accordingly, since 1990, several important international meetings have been held under UN auspices. For example, conferences and world "summits" on the future of our planet Earth (*Rio de Janeiro, 1992*), Human Rights (*Vienna, 1993*), Population and Development (*Cairo, 1994)*, Women (*Beijing, 1995*), Social Development (*Copenhagen, 1995 and Geneva, 2000*), Human Settlements (*Istanbul, 1996*), Commercial Exploitation of Children (*Stockholm, 1996*) Children and Youth (*Lisbon 1998, New York, 2002*) Crime Prevention (*Vienna, 2000*), The Millennium Summit (*New York, 2000*), AIDS (*New York, 2001*), Racism (*Durban, 2001*) Ageing (*Madrid, 2002*), Sustainable Development (*Johannesburg, 2002*), World Food Summit (*Rome, 2002*).

All these international gatherings at which States are represented by ministers - or often by heads of State or government, hence their designation as "summits" - aim to establish priorities for the 21st century.

For more than 50 years the United Nations has been, and continues to be active in every domain in which Member States need to cooperate, or require assistance from the international community.

Today, the United Nations efforts are, for the most part, concentrated in four main areas: the preservation of peace, humanitarian assistance, economic and social development, and human rights.

Mine clearance

Maintaining peace

From the earliest days of the Organization up to the end of the 1980s the United Nations was often paralyzed by continuous hostilities – the notorious "cold war" – between western nations and the former Soviet bloc. Most of the important initiatives affecting the interests of the great powers were blocked by a veto cast by one or other of the five permanent members of the Security Council.

Nevertheless, the UN was able to play an important role in ending the war in the Congo (1964), in the conflict between Iran and Iraq (1988) and in the withdrawal of Soviet troops from Afghanistan (1989). It was also instrumental in defusing dangerous crises, such as those that occurred over Berlin (1949), Cuba (1962) and the Middle East (1973).

With the end of the cold war, a new spirit of cooperation between the great powers has emerged, enabling them to reach agreement more readily on interventions by the UN. When a conflict arises, they are now more inclined to pool their efforts in trying to settle the conflict peacefully and in convincing the opponents to accept a UN "peace-keeping operation".

Did you know that...

The United Nations played a major role in the fight against apartheid*, up to the establishment of a democratic, non-racial form of Government in South Africa in 1995.

In the countries in which it intervenes, the UN attempts, first of all, to bring about an end to the fighting. Next it strives to help restore lasting peace.

BLUE HELMETS OBSERVING CEASE-FIRE.

Did you know that...

Over the years a number of major issues have been largely resolved; for example, colonialism. More than 80 countries gained their independence through decolonization, a movement for which the United Nations was the driving force.

Traditionally, United Nations peace-keepers, widely known as "blue helmets" or "blue berets" because of their distinctive headgear, have patrolled buffer zones between hostile parties, monitored ceasefires and helped defuse local conflicts, allowing the search for durable political settlements to continue. Althouh military personnel and structure remain the backbone of most operations, increasingly, peace-keepers include civilian police officers, deminers, human rights monitors and specialists in civil affairs and communications. Several UN missions have been asked to help organize elections and even to assume temporary administration of certain territories.

Peace-keeping operations have not always been successful; the UN has suffered setbacks, as for instance in Rwanda and in the former Yugoslavia. But there have also been very effective operations, such as in Namibia, Cambodia, Mozambique and East Timor.

The Security Council has not been able to avert the outbreak of war in all cases. The deployment of the Blue Helmets has at least made it possible to offer protection to civilian populations and to save countless lives.

The UN has no standing army. In every instance, when the Security Council decides on a peace-keeping operation, the UN invites Member States that have no direct interests in the area of conflict to place troops under its overall command.

The numbers of Blue Helmets deployed range from a few dozen to tens of thousands, depending on the nature of the mission. Over 40,000 were sent to the former Yugoslavia. There are currently some 15 peace-keeping missions in operation around the world.

While 13 operations were established in the first 40 years, 42 new operations have been launched since 1988. At its peak in 1993, the total deployment of UN military and civilian personnel reached more than 80,000 from 77 countries (46,445 from 87 countries in March 2002).

Mine clearance has become an important part of peace-keeping and humanitarian operations as thousands of civilians continue to be killed or maimed by the estimated 100 million landmines scattered across the globe. The United Nations was closely associated with efforts leading to the adoption of an international Convention on the elimination of anti-personnel mines and is also coordinating the clearance of landmines from former battlefields in Africa, Asia and Central America.

Experience has shown that just avoiding military conflicts is not sufficient for establishing a secure and lasting peace. It has led the UN to focus as never before on peace-building action to support structures and institutions that will strengthen and consolidate peace.

Did you know that...

From the first peace-keeping operation in 1948, up to March 2002, 1,731 people employed by the UN - military and civilian - have died on these missions.

The United Nations strives above all to prevent the outbreak of conflicts between nations; this is called "preventive diplomacy".

Another area which has emerged as one of the main priorities is conflict prevention. It has been defined as one of the Millennium goals and identified as one of the Secretary-General's priorities for his second term.

The issue of disarmament has been another subject of continuing concern in negotiations and conferences convened at regular intervals at the UN. The results have been less spectacular in this area. Still, some landmark treaties have been worked out and ratified under the auspices of the UN, such as the Chemical Weapons Convention, the Biological Weapons Convention and the Treaty on the Non-Proliferation of Nuclear Weapons.

Did you know that...

UN peace-keeping operations are entirely financed by special contributions from Member States.

The United Nations has long been active in the fight against terrorism. Since the early 1960s, the UN and its specialized agencies have worked out a large number of international agreements to provide the legal basis for action against such acts. After the attacks of September 11, 2001 on the United States, the United Nations has devoted urgent attention to the growing threats of terrorism around the world. In particular, the Security Council appealed to all States in the strongest terms, to step up measures they are taking to combat terrorism, and to keep the Council regularly informed of their cooperation.

UN AMBULANCES IN THE STREETS OF VUKOVAR (CROATIA).

Humanitarian assistance

The UN plays an important role in providing humanitarian assistance, often in conflict-ridden countries, inseparable from its peace-keeping efforts. It also has a significant programme for helping refugees, which is primarily the responsibility of the UN High Commissioner for Refugees (UNHCR).

High Commissioner for Refugees.

Established in 1951 with headquarters in Geneva, the Office of the UNHCR is currently assisting about 22 million people around the world. (In 1995 it helped over 27 million refugees who were in need). This figure represents one out of every 264 people on earth and includes refugees as well as persons displaced by war within their own countries, who were forced to leave their homes, often their families and their possessions, in fear of losing their lives or their freedom.

Did you know that...

In 2002 the UNHCR budget amounted to about $1.9 billion, financed almost entirely by voluntary contributions from Governments, non-governmental organizations and individuals. The United States, the European Union and Japan provided nearly half of the total.

Blue Helmets protecting civilians.

REFUGEES CAMP
© HCR

Wars between nations, but also civil wars, are the root cause of the massive uprooting of populations. Their plight is one of the greatest human tragedies of our time.

UNHCR's role is, above all, to protect the refugees against all violence which threatens their existence, including the forcible return to their homelands. It also provides them with food, shelter and needed medical care. When fighting comes to an end, UNHCR encourages and organizes the voluntary repatriation of refugees.

If such repatriation is not possible, the High Commissioner's Office helps the refugees to settle in the country where they sought asylum, or in another country. A programme as vast as this needs large sums of money and the resources available are always insufficient to meet the ever growing demands for assistance.

Did you know that...

Wars in the former Yugoslavia, Afghanistan and the Caucasus and the genocide* in Rwanda have caused the influx of millions of refugees into neighbouring countries.

CAMBODIAN REFUGEES ASSISTED BY UNHCR.

In order to improve the delivery of emergency humanitarian and relief assistance in countries stricken by war or natural disasters, an Office for the Coordination of Humanitarian Affairs was established within the UN Secretariat. Financed by an emergency relief fund, the Office is also in charge of monitoring the implementation of Security Council decisions on these matters.

Several other organizations and programmes of the United Nations "system" also carry out important humanitarian assistance projects.

Did you know that...

Approximately one fifth of the world's population now lives on less than one dollar a day.

Economic and social development

Peace-keeping operations and aid to refugees are the most visible, and certainly the most widely known, activities of the UN. But they must not obscure the important work carried out by the Organization, year after year for promoting economic development and social progress, as well as protecting health and the environment.

THE UNITED NATIONS DEVELOPMENT FUND FOR WOMEN.

These practical action programmes – which represent about 80 per cent of UN activities – are designed for the most part to benefit developing countries, helping them improve their technical capabilities and, increasingly, to meet their basic human and social needs. They have had a profound impact on the lives of millions of people.

The UN does not act alone. The specialized agencies join in a common, coordinated effort, particularly in countries that benefit from international assistance.

Did you know that...

Agreements worked out by the United Nations have made it possible to reduce by 30 per cent atmospheric pollution in Europe caused by sulphur.

Did you know that...

Irreplaceable ancient monuments, such as the Acropolis in Athens, the Temple of Abu Simbel in Egypt and Borobudur in Indonesia have been saved from ruin or destruction by UNESCO.

The Acropolis in Athens, Greece.

Thus, the ILO has the main responsibility for activities concerning employment, training, working conditions and social legislation. FAO works to improve the production and distribution of food and to promote rural development. WHO aims to help all people attain the highest possible levels of health and focuses on the eradication of major communicable diseases. UNESCO's efforts focus on the improvement of education for all, the training of teachers, the preservation of historic and cultural sites and the promotion of scientific research.

Smallpox was eradicated from the face of the earth thanks to campaigns coordinated by the World Health Organization (WHO).

Special programmes are funded through voluntary contributions by Member States to promote economic and social development. The United Nations Development Programme (UNDP) is the most important of these.

The United Nations Children's Fund.

Did you know that...

The elimination of child labour is one of the major programmes of the International Labour Organization.

In addition, special purpose funds have been created to finance activities in certain priority areas: assistance to children, the advancement of women, and the protection of the environment.

Among them the United Nations Children's Fund (UNICEF) plays a major role in improving the lives of children and mothers the world over.

Did you know that...

Since the 1950s numerous declarations of principles and strategic plans have been adopted by the United Nations.

■ *Human rights*

The protection of basic human rights, of the dignity and worth of the human person, and of the equal rights of men and women are given pride of place in the Charter. It is therefore natural that the UN should assign top priority to these concerns.

On 10 December 1948 the United Nations adopted the Universal Declaration of Human Rights, which was to become the foundation for all subsequent UN action in this domain.The year 1998 marked the fiftieth anniversary of this historic event, celebrated by all Member States. The Declaration proclaims that *"all human beings are born free and equal in dignity and in rights... without distinction of any kind, such as race, colour, sex, language, religion, political or other opinion, national or social origin, property, birth or other status."* The Declaration is called "universal" to signify that the values it proclaims apply to everyone, everywhere in the world.

The Universal Declaration of Human Rights spells out the civil, political, economic, social and cultural rights for all human beings: for example, freedom of expression, assembly and thought, and the right to education.

In order to facilitate the implementation of the Declaration, the UN has negotiated two international Covenants on human rights, one on economic, social and cultural rights and the other on civil and political rights, both of which entered into force in 1976. By signing the Covenants, States legally accept to abide by their provisions. So far only some 145 States (of the 191 UN members) have ratified the covenants. Unfortunately, this shows that not all Governments are prepared to accept these important, basic principles, aimed at ensuring a peaceful life for communities and individuals.

Other international conventions, binding on the States that ratify them, have been concluded on a wide range of important issues, such as the elimination of all forms of racial discrimination, the rights of the child, and against torture.

The High Commissioner for Human Rights, who coordinates all UN human rights activities, works with Governments to improve their observance of human rights, seeks to prevent violations and investigates abuses.

A Commission on Human Rights was established as early as 1946 to monitor the implementation of the Declaration and report on violations that occur anywhere in the world. The Commission, composed of 53 Member States, meets every year for six weeks in Geneva. Its work is always highly publicized.

Every year the Commission receives thousands of complaints of human rights violations. If, after examining the complaints, the Commission finds that the problems are severe, it can call for investigations by experts or "special rapporteurs". Such investigations were carried out, for example, in Rwanda, the former Yugoslavia, Iran, Iraq, Sudan and the Occupied Arab Territories. Reports are then drawn up and adopted by the Commission in public meetings.

Did you know that...

Since its founding, the UN has focused on the improvement of the status of women through legislation, notably the adoption of the Convention on the Elimination of Discrimination against Women, and through policies and programmes that integrate women in all aspects of economic and social life.

The reports of the Commission on Human Rights, along with its recommendations, are sent to the Governments of the countries accused of abuses. The publicity surrounding these reports gives them great moral authority but the UN does not have a mechanism to compel States found guilty of violations to carry out the recommendations and improve their human rights practices. The only means at the UN's disposal is the pressure of public opinion from the international community. This is not sufficient, certainly, but it is by no means insignificant.

The resolve to penalize the most flagrant violations of human rights led to the establishment of international criminal tribunals for the former Yugoslavia (1992) and for Rwanda (1995). They are charged with prosecuting persons accused of genocide and, in general, of flagrant abuses of international humanitarian law during the civil wars which had raged in those countries. In 1998 the United Nations set up the first permanent International Criminal Court as an autonomous institution, which, in the future, will prosecute such crimes wherever they occur around the world.

How much does the United Nations cost?

There is a tendency now and again to characterize the UN as a bottomless pit, where financing is concerned. The reality is very different. Here are some facts and figures that will put the costs in perspective.

■ *The annual budget of the UN*

The UN spends $1.3 billion per year for its core functions – the Secretariat operations in New York, Geneva and every other part of the world where the UN is present. This is only about 4 per cent of the annual budget of New York City. The city of Tokyo spends $1.8 billion just to cover the cost of its fire department.

Some 61.000 people work in the UN system. This includes the UN Secretariat in New York, Geneva and other duty stations, as well as the staff of the other organizations around the world. In comparison, the World Disney Company, a multinational corporation, has almost twice the number of employees and, globally, McDonald's restaurants have three times as many.

■ *The annual cost of peace-keeping operations*

The cost of peace-keeping in 2002 was approximately $2.75 billion – the equivalent of less than 0.75 per cent of the US military budget and less than 0.3 per cent of the world's military spending.

■ *The annual budget of the UN system's operational activities*

The United Nations and its agencies, funds and programmes (excluding the financial institutions, such as the World Bank and the International Monetary Fund) have $4.8 billion a year to spend on economic, social and humanitarian assistance to the world's poorest countries. This is the equivalent of 80 cents per inhabitant on this planet. By contrast, in 1996 the world's Governments spent about $797 billion for military purposes - or about $135 per individual.

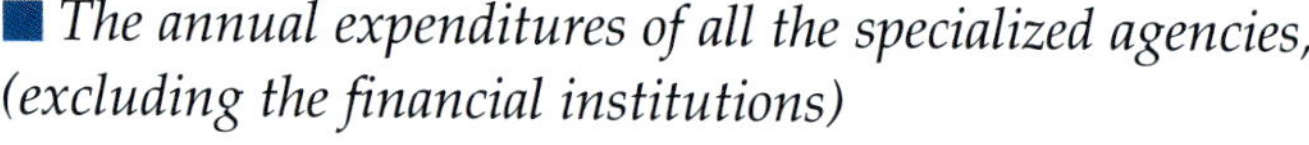

■ *The annual expenditures of all the specialized agencies, (excluding the financial institutions)*

The money spent by the UN, its agencies and Government delegations contribute $3.2 billion a year to the economy of the New York City area.

Taken together, these expenditures amount to $1.8 billion a year, barely more than the public health budget of a country like France. If these figures seem high it is because they cover activities on a world-wide scale. In fact, the share paid by each contributing country represents only a very small part of its national budget. Considering the scope of the work carried out, the costs incurred by the UN system are really modest. The funds available are also quite inadequate to meet the continuously growing demand for UN assistance.

■ *Who pays?*

All the countries that belong to the UN pay for its budget. The share of each State is determined by its ability to pay and is proportionate to its national income. Hence the rich countries are the major contributors to the UN. Nine countries cover more than 75 per cent of the Organization's expenditures. In 2001 they ranked as follows: the United States (22 per cent), Japan (19.6 per cent), Germany (9.8 per cent), France (6.5 per cent), Italy (5.1 per cent), the United Kingdom (5.1 per cent), Canada (2.6 per cent), Spain (2.5 per cent) and Brazil (2.2 per cent).

When States are ranked according to a different order, namely the amount of their "per citizen" contributions, a different picture emerges: the USA's share of $1.11 per tax payer stands in contrast to, for example, Sweden's $1.57, and tiny San Marino's $4.75.

■ *Financial problems*

Time and again the UN has been plagued with serious shortages of money. A number of Governments do not pay their contributions on time, causing a continuously recurring financial crisis in the Organization. Consequently, the UN and the other organizations of the UN system are frequently forced to cut programmes urgently needed by the countries and populations whom they were designed to benefit. Also, much like private companies, these organizations must often reduce their staff.

The United Nations today and tomorrow

Rarely, if ever, have the people of this earth placed such high hopes and bold dreams in a world organization. The fiftieth anniversary of the United Nations and the Millenium Summit offered an occasion to evaluate the results achieved since its founding and to pave the way for the future.

■ *The limitations*

There has been criticism of the Organization but one must bear in mind that the UN's "performance" depends much more on the political will of Member States to work together, than on the competence of the Secretary-General or the Secretariat.

For example, it would be fitting for the richest member countries to give to the UN the necessary resources to help the poorest. In reality most tend to provide this help directly, rather than through an international organization, in order to expand their political influence. Moreover, there are matters in which Governments are reluctant to accept intervention by the international community: for example, in human rights or disarmament questions.

■ *The weak points*

In the course of the years the administration of the UN has become unwieldy. However, a series of reforms recently put in place have resulted in the streamlining of Secretariat offices and the introduction of new efficiency measures.

■ *Recognized accomplishments*

Meanwhile, the UN has been more active than ever since the late 1980s. It has achieved significant results, for example, in peace-keeping, humanitarian assistance and development aid. Thus, by gradually gaining the right to intervene within countries when dangerous conflicts erupt, the UN has been able to save countless lives. Furthermore, the UN system's track record with practical assistance programmes in developing countries is second to none. These programmes have reduced the suffering from hunger and disease of the most

Did you know that...

Years before 2001 when the UN and its Secretary-General were awarded the Nobel Peace Price, several organizations and programmes in the UN System have been similarly honoured for outstanding service : the UN Peace-keeping Forces (1988), the United Nations High Commissioner for Refugees (1954 and 1981), the International Labour Organization (1969) and UNICEF (1965).

Did you know that...

Sustainable development recognizes the essential links between the balanced use of natural resources, economic growth, social justice and environmental protection.

vulnerable groups and generally helped improve the lives of millions of people in the poorest parts of the world. They touch on all areas critical to our well-being and range from the establishment of universal human rights standards to the improvement of education, health and the environment.

A plan of action for the future

In September 2000, by solemnly approving the "Millennium Declaration", unanimously adopted by the General Assembly, Member States agreed on a plan of action for the future. They pledged to meet the following major goals by the year 2015 : Eradicate extreme poverty and hunger ; Achieve universal primary education ; Promote equality between men and women ; Reduce child mortality ; Improve maternal health ; Combat HIV / AIDS, malaria and other major diseases ; Integrate the principles of sustainable development into country policies ; Develop a global partnership for development. These goals are to be the guidelines for national and international action in the coming years.

Further information about the UN and its activities may be obtained from the UN Information Centres in individual countries, from the UN Public Inquiries Units :

United Nations - New York, NY 10017 ;

United Nations Office at Geneva - CH 1211 Geneva 10 ;

or from the UN Home Page on the Internet World Wide Web (http://www.un.org).

An irreplaceable organization

Do we need the United Nations today as much as we did in 1945? The answer is an unqualified "yes"! Without this unique forum for continuing dialogue the conflicts that arise around the world would surely escalate, as there would be no mechanism to exert pressure on the warring parties to negotiate.

When great calamities occur – wars or natural disasters – who would bring massive humanitarian aid to the victims? Would human rights abuses not become even more flagrant without a world organization to bear witness and to condemn them? Could international development assistance, as delivered by the UN, without political strings attached, be allowed to disappear?

Indeed, if, suddenly, the Organization ceased to exist, it would surely have to be re-created. International public opinion must therefore offer the United Nations its full support. It must also give it encouragement to continue evolving and improving its ability to respond to the great challenges of our world in the twenty-first century.